CREATURES IN WHITE

ARCTIC WOLVES

For Andrew, who is fast, curious, and intelligent . . .
just like a wolf.

With thanks to Dr. David Mech, for sharing his expertise.
He is known throughout the world as the dean of wolf
researchers and has received the Wildlife Society's pres-
tigious Aldo Leopold Memorial Award.

Thanks also to Dr. John Weaver, Carnivore Conservation
Biologist, who has written three books on carnivores and
has had papers reviewed in six scientific jounals.

W.P.

Text copyright ©1997 by Wendy Pfeffer.

 Published by Silver Press
A Division of Simon & Schuster
299 Jefferson Road, Parsippany, NJ 07054

Designed by Brooks Design

Printed in the United States of America

ISBN 0-382-39320-1 (LSB) 10 9 8 7 6 5 4 3 2 1
ISBN 0-382-39319-8 (PBK) 10 9 8 7 6 5 4 3 2 1

Library of Congress Cataloging-in-Publication Data

Pfeffer, Wendy
Arctic wolves/by Wendy Pfeffer.
p. cm.–(Creatures in White)
Summary: Describes the life cycle of these hardy wolves that live in the High Arctic, where temperatures
can be as low as seventy degrees below zero.
1. Wolves—Arctic regions—Juvenile literature. [1. Wolves—Arctic regions.] I. Title. II. Series: Pfeffer, Wendy.
Creatures in White.
QL737.C22P478 1997 95-17833
599.74'442-dc 20 CIP AC

Photo credits: Photo research: Susan Van Etten; Cover, ©Zig Leszczynski/Animals, Animals; title page:
Joseph R. Pearce/DRK photo; p. 4-5, ©Dr. David Mech; 6-7, ©Stan Wayman/Photo Researcher, Inc.;
8-9, 10-11, 12-13, 14-15, 16-17, 18-19, 20-21, 22-23, 24-25, ©Dr. David Mech; 26-27, ©Renee
Lynn/Photo Researcher, Inc.; 28-29, ©Dr. David Mech; 30, top, ©Tom McHugh/Photo Reseachers, Inc.;
30, m, ©Zig Leszczynski/Animals, Animals; 30, b, ©Dr. David Mech; 31, ©Sandra Gaumont /Gaumont
Photography; end paper, ©Dr. David Mech; back cover, ©Dr. David Mech

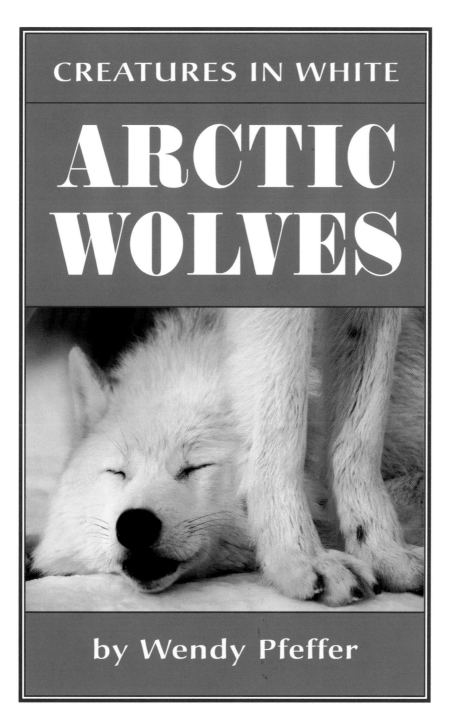

CREATURES IN WHITE

ARCTIC WOLVES

by Wendy Pfeffer

Enjoy these curious
"Creatures in White."
Love,
Wendy Pfeffer

Silver Press

Parsippany, New Jersey

1998

Far to the north, in a place called the High Arctic, wolf howls break the silence of the long winter's night. A pack of white wolves has wandered for several weeks without finding food.

The leader of the pack guides his family over a frozen wilderness. A cold north wind swirls around him and ruffles his thick white coat. His white-furred mate plods along next to him.

The leader guides his family to the top of a rocky ridge. Camouflaged in the snow below, some white arctic hares scratch out plant sprigs from under the snow. For just a moment, one hare stands on its hind legs. The alert wolves see it. They bound over crags and crevices down to the snowfield, racing toward their prey.

The hares run fast, zigzagging around snow-covered rocks. But the wolves don't tire easily. And they take shortcuts. After a long chase, the wolves catch and eat their prey.

A bitter cold wind howls in the darkness. It's 70 degrees below zero—not fit for human beings. But the wolves sleep outdoors, each curled in a tight white ball with its bushy tail over its nose. Thick white fur protects their bodies from cold and acts like white leggings to keep their legs and toes warm.

After the long, cold, dark winter, the sun appears for the first time in five months. The female finds a cave in the rocky ledge. She crawls inside and gives birth to five pups. They're safe in their den. Its opening is too small for a hungry polar bear to squeeze in.

The father waits outside the den and listens carefully. Another wolf in the family listens, too. When they hear the pups whimper, they know the pups have been born. So they wag their tails at the news.

The mother licks her pups clean with her long wide tongue. She snuggles them to her warm, white, furry body and lets them drink her rich milk. She looks at her pups' tiny ears, their short fuzzy legs, and big round heads. Her helpless pups cannot see or hear. Each pup is about the size of a small loaf of bread.

For the first few weeks the father brings food to the mother. Just outside the cave, he leaves hares or small, fat, furry rodents called lemmings.

After about one week the pups begin to crawl, dragging their bellies on the stone floor of the den. Their heads dangle like rag dolls.

At two weeks the pups' eyes open. They can see. They can hold their heads up, too.

At three weeks the pups come out of the den for the first time. They curl up on the ground and nuzzle close to their mother.

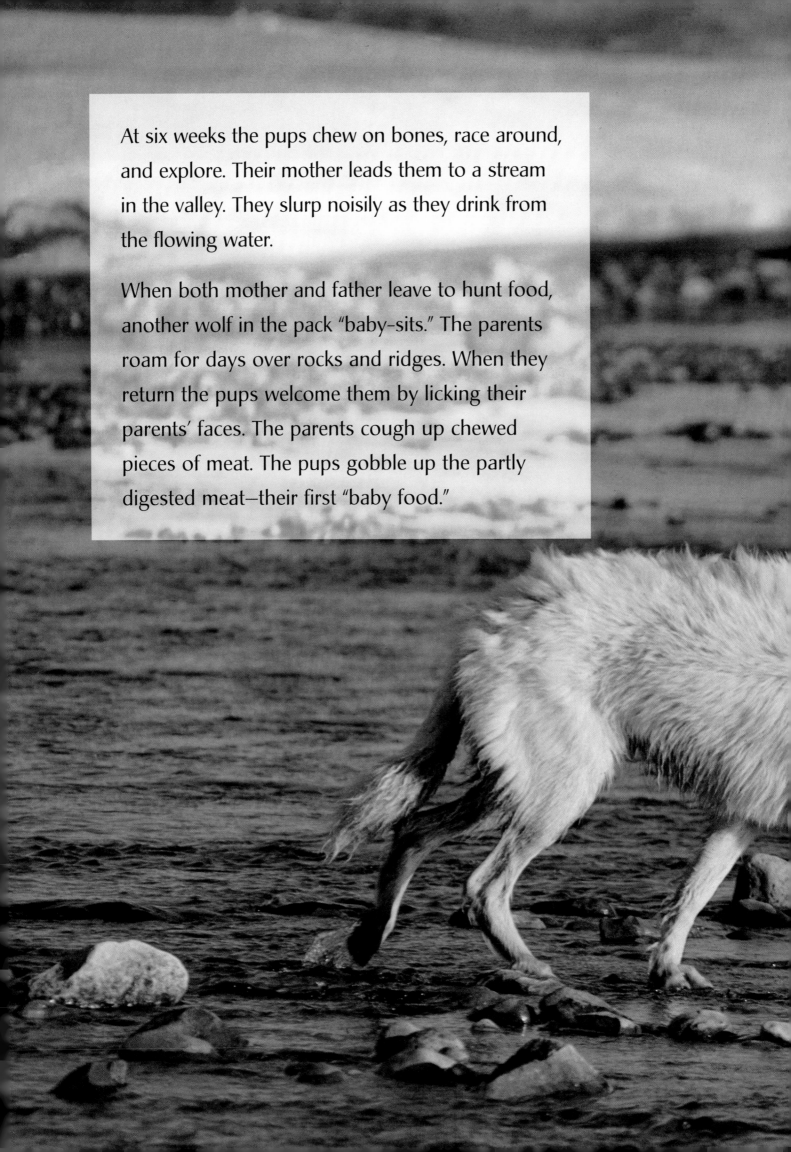

At six weeks the pups chew on bones, race around, and explore. Their mother leads them to a stream in the valley. They slurp noisily as they drink from the flowing water.

When both mother and father leave to hunt food, another wolf in the pack "baby-sits." The parents roam for days over rocks and ridges. When they return the pups welcome them by licking their parents' faces. The parents cough up chewed pieces of meat. The pups gobble up the partly digested meat—their first "baby food."

The other wolves greet their leader by crouching down before him, with ears back and tails between their legs, to show their respect for him.

From April to August the sun shines all day and all night. Dwarf willows sprout. Yellow poppies burst into bloom. And the eight-week-old pups wrestle and romp together. The adult wolves' thick white coats begin to shed. Birds dip down and gather the white puffs for their nests.

A long-tailed bird, called a jaeger, dives down, pestering the mother wolf, as if to say, "Stay away from my nest." Since the mother wolf can't catch the jaeger, she shows her wolflings how to run through valleys, nose in lemming holes, and leap over mounds of rocky earth.

The pups move like shadows, learning to stalk small prey. They're almost ready to catch their own. While snowy owls hoot and hunt rodents, the pups listen for other sounds, like the squeak of a lemming or the chirp of a bird.

By late fall the pups are strong. Their furry coats have grown thick and long and are beginning to turn white. The pups run with the pack. But sometimes the curious wolflings wander. Howls keep them in touch with their family.

Far from the pups, the leader lifts his head skyward and howls. Other wolves join in. The pups' heads go up. Their ears lay back. Their voices merge with the musical sounds drifting across the meadows and mountaintops of the vast Arctic tundra.

In autumn, snow falls more often. The wolflings lick the snowflakes off their furry shoulders as a herd of huge shaggy musk oxen wanders into the valley below.

The musk oxen graze on grasses growing there. The leader of the wolf pack spots them. The pack must take care. Musk oxen are dangerous animals. They kick with their hoofs and stab with their sharp-pointed horns.

The wolves approach carefully. The shaggy musk oxen see the wolves and form a circle, heads and horns facing out. The calves run into the circle for protection. The wolves dart in and out, then they attack and send the oxen running. With the circle broken, the wolves chase a calf away from the herd, then capture it.

The parents eat as much as they want. Then the wolflings eat. The parents hold off the other wolves for a while, then let them eat their fill. Leftover meat gets buried to use later, when food is scarce. It won't spoil in the frozen ground— nature's refrigerator.

During their first winter, the pups grow to full size. They roam with the pack over their cold, dark, snow-covered territory searching for food.

In early spring when the wolflings are about a year old, they have enough skills to go out on their own. Some wolflings stay with the pack. Others grow restless and leave. Each travels far until it finds a mate in a new area. They form a bond with each other. The next spring they produce pups.

Some of these pups will learn skills in the summer to survive the long, cold, dark winter and live to see the sun shine again in the spring.

Whatever the season, arctic wolves wander and howl. Their voices ring through the air and float over the cold windblown plains of their home, the High Arctic.

Wolf Facts

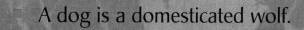

- A dog is a domesticated wolf.

- Adult wolves range in size from 50 to 170 pounds.

- A fully grown wolf's paw is the size of a man's fist or larger.

- A wolf pack is usually six or seven male and female wolves but it can be as few as two or as many as thirty.

- Wolves in the wild may live eleven to thirteen years.

- Wolves not only howl, whimper, and snarl, they also woof, bark, whine, squeak, and growl.

- A wolf's sense of smell may be one hundred times greater than a person's.

- Wolves eat any kind of meat, from a tiny mouse to a huge moose. An adult wolf can eat twenty pounds of meat at one feeding. That's equal to eighty hamburgers or a large turkey.

- Arctic wolves are all white. Other wolves can be almost any color: red, black, cream, brown, or gray. Gray and black are the most common colors.

- There is no record of a healthy wild wolf ever killing a human being in the United States.

- Wolves are a vital part of nature. To get more information on the role they play contact:

  The International Wolf Center

  1396 Highway 169

  Ely, MN 55731–8129 USA

  1–800–Ely Wolf or 218–365–4695

  Web page address http://www.wolf.org

WHERE IN THE WORLD
ARE ARCTIC WOLVES?

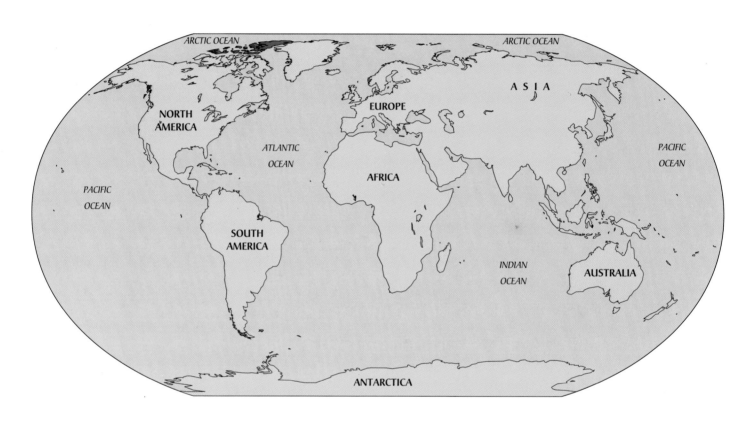

Arctic Wolves live here